SUPER SIMPLE

FAIRY GARDENS

A KID'S GUIDE TO GARDENING

ALEX KUSKOWSKI

Super Sandcastle

An Imprint of Abdo Publishing
www.abdopublishing.com

Consulting Editor, Diane Craig,
M.A./Reading Specialist

www.abdopublishing.com

Published by Abdo Publishing, a division of ABDO, PO Box 398166, Minneapolis, Minnesota 55439. Copyright © 2015 by Abdo Consulting Group, Inc. International copyrights reserved in all countries. No part of this book may be reproduced in any form without written permission from the publisher. Super SandCastle™ is a trademark and logo of Abdo Publishing.

Printed in the United States of America, North Mankato, Minnesota
102014
012015

THIS BOOK CONTAINS RECYCLED MATERIALS

Editor: Liz Salzmann
Content Developer: Alex Kuskowski
Cover and Interior Design and Production: Mighty Media, Inc.
Photo Credits: Jen Schoeller, Shutterstock

Library of Congress Cataloging-in-Publication Data

Kuskowski, Alex.
  Super simple fairy gardens : a kid's guide to gardening / Alex Kuskowski.
    pages cm. -- (Super simple gardening)
  ISBN 978-1-62403-522-7
1. Gardens, Miniature--Juvenile literature. I. Title. II. Series: Kuskowski, Alex. Super simple gardening.
  SB433.5.K87 2015
  635.9--dc23
                    2014023617

Super SandCastle™ books are created by a team of professional educators, reading specialists, and content developers around five essential components—phonemic awareness, phonics, vocabulary, text comprehension, and fluency—to assist young readers as they develop reading skills and strategies and increase their general knowledge. All books are written, reviewed, and leveled for guided reading, early reading intervention, and Accelerated Reader® programs for use in shared, guided, and independent reading and writing activities to support a balanced approach to literacy instruction.

TO ADULT HELPERS

Gardening is a lifelong skill. It is fun and simple to learn. There are a few things to remember to keep kids safe. Gardening requires commitment. Help your children stay dedicated to watering and caring for their plants. Some activities in this book recommend adult supervision. Some use sharp tools. Be sure to review the activities before starting and be ready to assist your budding gardeners when necessary.

Key Symbols

In this book you may see these symbols. Here is what they mean.

Hot!
You will be working with something hot. Get help.

Inside Light
Put your plant inside.

Outside Light
Put your plant outside.
Direct Light = in sunlight.
Indirect Light = in shade.

TABLE OF CONTENTS

A BIT OF GARDEN MAGIC

Dig into the world of gardening! Make a fairy garden full of magic and wonder. Fairies love to play in gardens, and you will too!

It is easy to start. This book will give you simple tips. Learn about the plants you can grow. Get your hands dirty. Grow something great!

FAIRY GARDENS

Fairy gardens are tiny gardens. Plant a fairy garden to invite in the garden fairies. Include **details** such as small homes or tiny furniture.

START SPROUTING

Fairy gardens take time and attention.
Start planning your fairy garden.
Learn how to take care of it.

Inside Gardens

Fairy gardens need a safe place. Put the plants where the temperature stays the same. Make sure to water your indoor fairy garden.

Outside Gardens

Outside fairy gardens take planning! Learn about the plants you want to use. Some outdoor plants grow better in certain areas.

TOOLS

These are some of the important gardening tools you will be using for the projects in this book.

containers & pots

garden gloves

hand trowel

plants

soil & sand

rocks

watering can

moss

SAFETY

Be safe and responsible while gardening. There are a few rules for doing gardening projects.

Ask Permission

Get **permission** to do a project. You might want to use tools or things around the house. Ask first!

Be Safe

Get help from an adult when using sharp tools or moving something heavy.

Clean Up

Clean up your working area when you are finished. Put everything away.

DIG INTO DIRT

Fairy gardens need a lot of flowers and plants. Keep the plants you get healthy by using the right soil.

Choose the best soil for your plants. If you don't know, ask a gardener for help.

Desert Potting Mix
This soil works best with **cacti** and other **succulents**.

All-Purpose Potting Mix
This soil works well with most plants in pots. Buy soil with **peat moss** and **vermiculite**.

ADD IT!

Rocks

Some pots need rocks in the bottom. This helps the water drain out of the soil. It keeps the roots from getting too wet.

Fertilizer

Fertilizer is food for plants! Most plants need fertilizer every few weeks. It comes in **pellets**, powder, or liquid. The package will tell you how much to use.

LOCATION STATION

Find a Spot

Putting your plants in the right place is important! Choose a spot with the right amount of sun.

Pick a Pot

Containers for plants come in all shapes, sizes, and **materials**. Try colorful plastic pots or fun clay pots.

Use the Right Size Pot

Plants need room to grow! The roots should not touch the sides of the pot.

TIP

Some pots have holes in the bottom. This helps drain extra water. They should be placed on **saucers** to catch the water.

Small Pots
Pots less than
8 inches (20 cm) deep.

Medium Pots
Pots 8 inches (20 cm) to
16 inches (40.5 cm) deep.

Large Pots
Pots deeper than
16 inches (40.5 cm).

COOL CARE

Watering Wisdom

Plants need water. Keep the soil moist for most plants. If the soil feels dry, water your plants!

The Right Light

Light is important! Get the right light for your plants. Check how many hours of sunlight your plants need.

To get the right light inside, know what direction the windows face. South facing windows give the most light. East and west facing windows have a medium amount of light. North facing windows have the least light.

HOME SWEET HOME

Make your fairy garden inviting for the fairies. Add a tiny house, table, or walkway. They will make the fairies feel right at home!

▸ **A small fairy house**

▸ **Fairy-sized tables and chairs**

▸ **A tiny fence**

▸ **A fairy walkway**

▸ **Fake toadstools and plants**

FLOWERS FOR FAIRIES

ATTRACT FAIRIES WITH A TINY PARK!

OUTSIDE
DIRECT SUN

Supplies

- potting soil
- large terra-cotta pot
- ruler
- hand trowel
- garden gloves
- 2 zinnia seedlings
- 2 petunia seedlings
- 2 kale seedlings
- small rocks
- dried moss
- glass pebbles
- tiles
- small sticks, 1 inch (2.5 cm) long
- yellow string
- garden gnome (see pages 28 to 29)

DIRECTIONS

1. Put potting soil in the pot. Fill the pot to 3 inches (7.5 cm) from the top.

2. Dig a hole near the side. Dig about 3 inches (7.5 cm) deep.

3. Take the zinnias out of their trays. Pull gently at the roots to loosen them.

4. Place the zinnias in the hole. Cover the roots with soil. Press down on the soil.

Project continues on the next page

5 Dig a second hole a few inches away. Plant the petunia seedlings in the hole.

6 Plant the kale seedlings the same way.

7 Cover the dirt around the zinnias with small rocks. Make a circle around the plants.

8 Cover the rest of the dirt with moss. To shape it, pull the moss apart gently. Press it into the soil where it is needed.

9 Put glass pebbles around the small rocks. Add tiles for stepping-stones.

10 Put sticks in the soil every ½ inch (1.3 cm) around the edge of the pot.

11 Tie string to a stick. Wind the string in between the sticks. Go around the pot two times. Tie the string to a stick when finished.

12 Add a garden **gnome**. Water all the plants well.

COOL CARE

Put the garden where it gets sun part of the day. Water two to three times a week. Add some fairy decorations.

BEACH GARDEN

TAKE A VACATION WITH THIS GARDEN!

INSIDE
INDIRECT SUN

Supplies

green metal bucket
rocks
garden gloves
hand trowel
potting soil
ruler
celosia seedlings
polka dot seedlings
sand
blue glass pebbles
small seashells
cardboard
scissors
acrylic paint
paintbrush
paper umbrella
garden gnome
(see pages 28 to 29)

DIRECTIONS

1. Put 2 inches (5 cm) of rocks in the bucket.

2. Put potting soil in the bucket. Fill it to 3 inches (7.5 cm) from the top.

3. Take the celosia seedlings out of the trays. Pull gently at the roots to loosen them. Place the seedlings on the dirt.

Project continues on the next page

4 Add soil to keep the celosia in place. Press down.

5 Take the polka dot seedlings out of the trays. Pull gently at the roots to loosen them.

6 Put the plant on the dirt. Add soil to keep it in place. Press down. Cover the soil with sand.

7 Cover part of the sand with blue glass pebbles.

8 Put seashells near the glass pebbles.

9 Decorate your beach. Add a garden **gnome**. Cut and paint cardboard to look like a surfboard. Add a paper beach umbrella.

10 Water your plants well!

COOL CARE Put the garden in a sunny area. Water the plants at least once a week.

ANIMAL GARDEN

LET THESE ANIMALS RUN WILD!

INSIDE
INDIRECT SUN

Supplies
• • • • • • • • •

large glass jar

rocks

dried moss

large bowl

garden gloves

hand trowel

potting soil

2½-inch (6.3 cm) succulent plant

Brazilian red hot seedling

measuring cup

plastic animals

DIRECTIONS

1. Put 1 inch (2.5 cm) of rocks in the jar.

2. Put the dried moss in a large bowl. Cover the moss with water. Let it **soak** 5 minutes.

3. Remove the moss. Squeeze out the extra water.

4. Flatten the moss. Cover the rocks with the moss.

Project continues on the next page

5. Add at least 3 inches (7.5 cm) of soil on top of the moss.

6. Dig a small hole near the edge of the jar.

7. Take the **succulent** out of its tray. Pull gently at the roots to loosen them. Put the plant in the hole.

8. Add soil to the jar. Push the soil around the succulent. Press down to make the soil firm.

9 Dig a hole near the other side of the jar.

10 Take the seedling out of its tray. Pull gently at the roots. Put the plant in the hole. Add more soil. Press down to make the soil firm around the plants.

11 Pull apart dried moss pieces. Place them over the soil.

12 Water the plants with 1 cup of water. Place the plastic animals in the jar.

COOL CARE

This garden needs a few hours of sun every day. Water it every 1 to 2 weeks, or when the soil is dry.

GARDEN FRILLS

MAKE ACCESSORIES FOR YOUR GARDEN!

Supplies
. . . .

CAUTION HOT!

oven-bake clay, red, green & tan

wooden birdhouse

acrylic paint

paintbrush

wooden sticks

ruler

craft glue

Garden Gnome

1. Shape red clay into a cone 1 inch (2.5 cm) high. Shape tan clay into a ball. Stick the bottom of the cone to the ball. This is the **gnome**'s head.

2. Make a roll of green clay 2 inches (5 cm) long for the body. Stick the head to the body.

3. Add arms. Stick a small circle of tan clay to each side of the body.

4. Combine all the clay colors. Make two small ovals. Stick them to the bottom of the body for shoes.

5. Bake the clay according to the directions on the package.

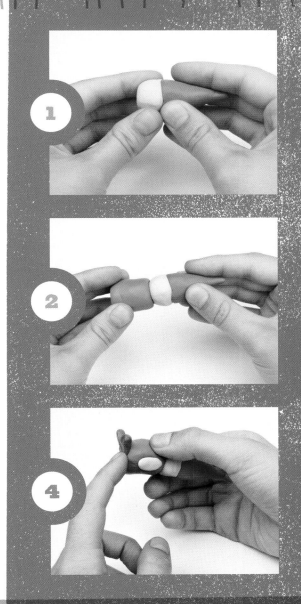

Sweet Fairy Home

1. Paint a door and two windows on the back of the birdhouse.

2. Cut some wooden sticks about 2.5 inches (6.3 cm) long.

3. Glue the sticks around the bottom of the birdhouse. Let the glue dry.

4. Glue moss to the roof of the birdhouse. Let the glue dry.

Fairy Bench

1. Make two rectangles out of clay. Make them 2 inches (5 cm) by 1 inch (2 cm).

2. Press the rectangles together. This forms the seat and back of the bench.

3. Make four small cubes ½ inch (1.3 cm) on each side. Press the cubes to the bottom of the bench seat.

4. Bake the clay according to the directions on the package.

5. Paint the bench. Let the paint dry.

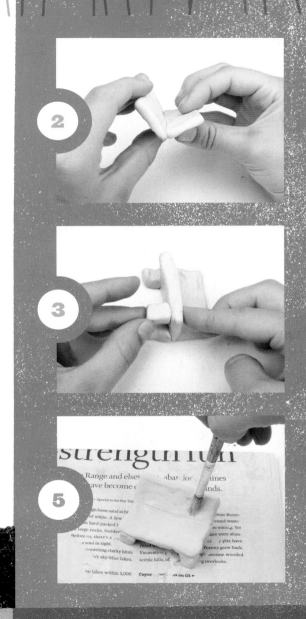

GLOSSARY

cactus – a plant with sharp spikes instead of leaves that grows in hot dry places.

container – something that other things can be put into.

detail – a small part of something.

fertilizer – something used to make plants grow better in soil.

gnome – a character from many folk legends that looks like a short, old man.

material – something that other things can be made of, such as clay, plastic, or metal.

peat moss – a type of moss that usually grows on wet land and is used in gardening.

pellet – a small, hard ball.

permission – when a person in charge says it's okay to do something.

saucer – a shallow dish that goes under something to catch spills.

soak – to remain covered in a liquid for a while.

succulent – a plant, such as a cactus or an aloe, that has thick stems or leaves that store water.

vermiculite – a light material that holds water that is often added to potting soil.